Macramé For Beginners

Many Easy Projects For Your Home

Copyright © 2020

All rights reserved.

DEDICATION

The author and publisher have provided this e-book to you for your personal use only. You may not make this e-book publicly available in any way. Copyright infringement is against the law. If you believe the copy of this e-book you are reading infringes on the author's copyright, please notify the publisher at: https://us.macmillan.com/piracy

Contents

easy Diy Macrame Wall Hanging 1

Simple Macrame Table Runner Diy 1

Macrame Plant Hanger Diy – A Friendship Bracelet For Plants

.... 1

How To Make This Diy Macrame Tote Bag Using Jute 13

Easy DIY Macrame Wall Hanging

A macrame wall hanging is an easy DIY project that will add a handmade touch to any room in your home. This free tutorial will help you create a wall hanging with a lot of interesting patterns, such as spirals and triangles. Don't be afraid to change it up to make it your own.

Despite how it looks, this is a simple project that will just take you an hour or two to complete. It really comes together fast and you'll find lots of opportunities to add your own style to it.

This is just one of many free macrame patterns that include plant hangers, bookmarks, curtains, and a whole lot more.

The knots you'll be using for this macrame wall hanging include Lark's Head knot, Spiral knot, and Square knot. You can learn how to tie all these knots by reading our guide on how to macrame.

What You'll Need

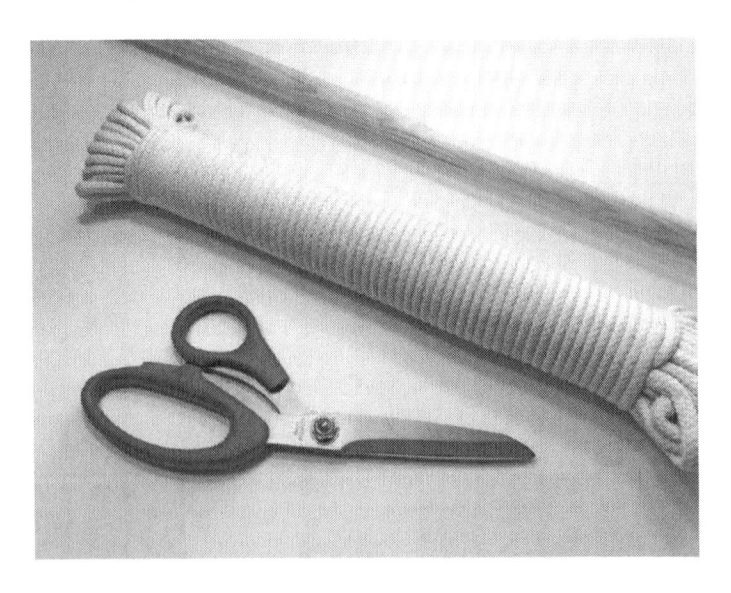

Here's what you'll need to complete this DIY macrame wall hanging:

Cotton Macrame Cord (200 feet or 61 meters)

Wooden Dowel (3/4-inch diameter, 24 inches long)

Scissors

I'm using cotton clothesline for my macrame cord. It has a wonderful natural look to it and is fairly inexpensive.

The wooden dowel doesn't need to be these exact dimensions and in place of the wooden dowel, use whatever size you like as long as you can fit all the ropes over it. If you'd like to give it a more outdoorsy feel, you could use a tree branch about the same size.

Make a Hanger for Your Wooden Dowel

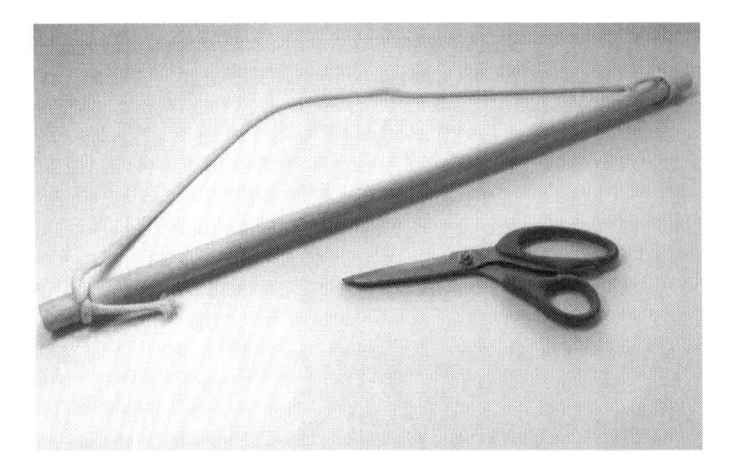

Cut a piece of macrame cord that's three feet (one meter). Tie each end of the cord to the two sides of the wooden dowel.

You'll use this to hang your macrame project when it's finished. I like to attach it at the beginning so I can hang the macrame project as I tie knots. Working this way is much easier than laying it down.

Cut Your Macrame Cord

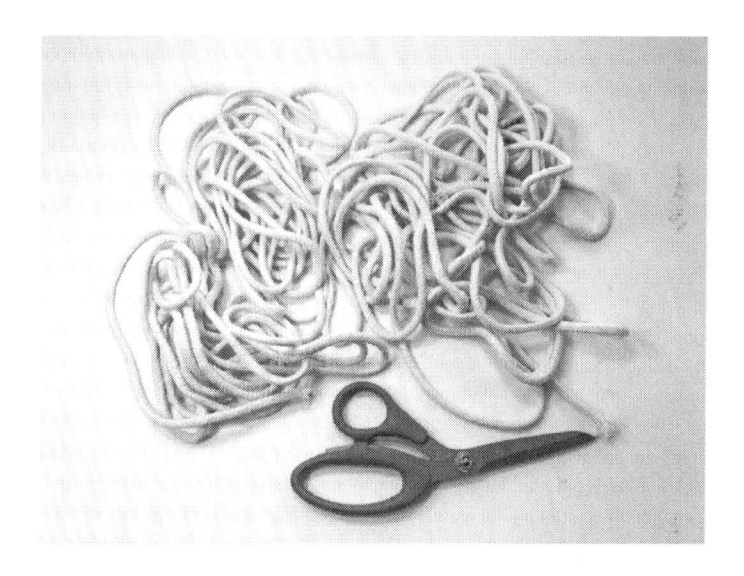

Cut your macrame cord into 12 lengths of rope that are 15 feet (4.5 meters) long.

This may seem like a lot of cord but knots take up more cord than you would think. There's no way to make your rope longer if you need to, so it's better to cut more than you'll use.

Attach Macrame Cord to Dowel

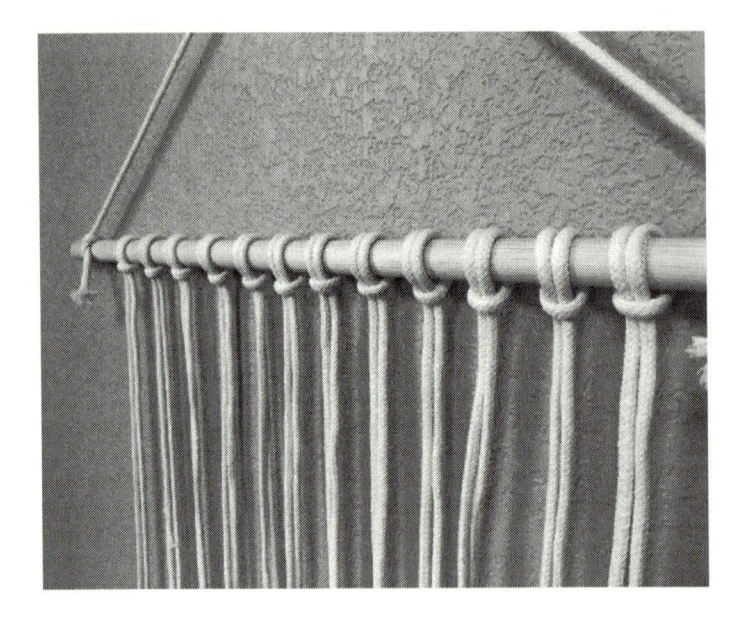

Fold one of the macrame cords in half and use a lark's head knot to attach it to the wooden dowel.

Attach all the other cords in the same way.

Knot Spiral Stitches

Take the first 4 cords and make a left-facing spiral stitch (also called a half knot sinnet) by tying 13 half knots.

Continue Knotting Spiral Stitches

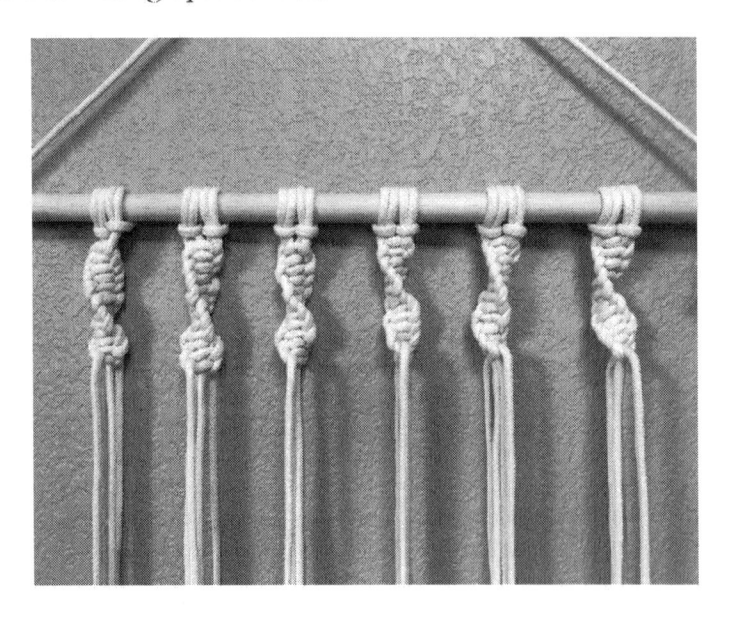

Use the next set of four ropes to make another spiral stitch with 13 half knots. Continue working in groups with four cords. When you finish, you should have a total of six spiral stitches.

Make Square Knots

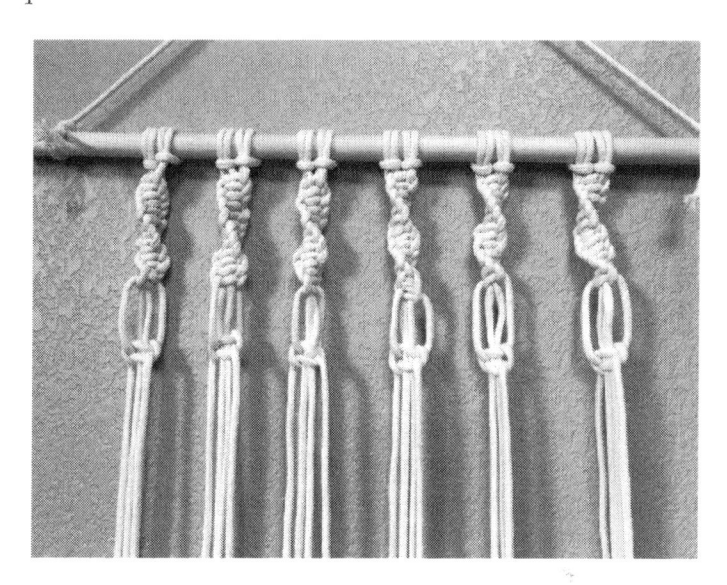

Measure approximately two inches down from the last knot in the spiral stitch. This is where you're going to place your next knot, the square knot.

Using the first four cords, make a right facing square knot. Continue making the right facing square knots all the way across this row. Do your best to keep them all horizontally even with each other. You'll end up with a set of six square knots.

Decrease Square Knots

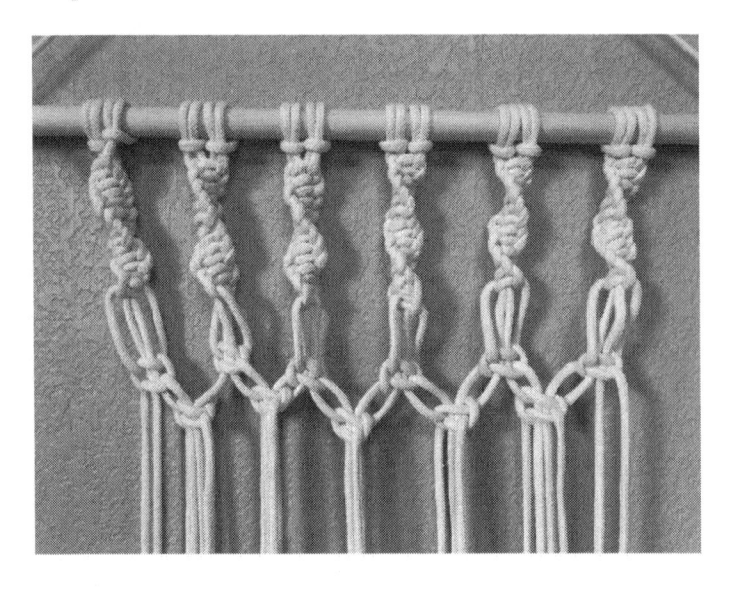

Now it's time to start decreasing the square knots so we can have a "V" shape of knots.

Leave the first two cords and the last two cords free. Make right facing square knots with each group of four. You'll now have a second row with the two first and two last cords unknotted and five square knots.

It doesn't matter how you space these, just keep them even with each other for each row.

Continue Deceasing the Square Knots

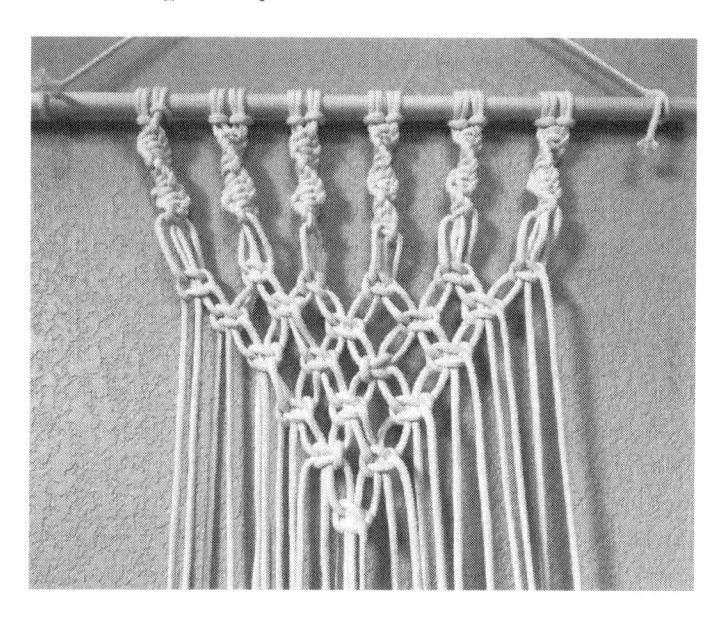

For the third row, you're going to leave out the first four cords and the last four cords. You'll have four square knots.

For the fourth row leave out six cords at the beginning and six cords at the end. You'll have three square knots.

In the fifth row, you'll leave out eight cords at the beginning and eight more cords at the end. You'll have two square knots now.

For the sixth and final row, you'll leave out 10 cords at the beginning and 10 cords at the end. This will leave you with four cords to make one final square knot.

Increase Square Knots

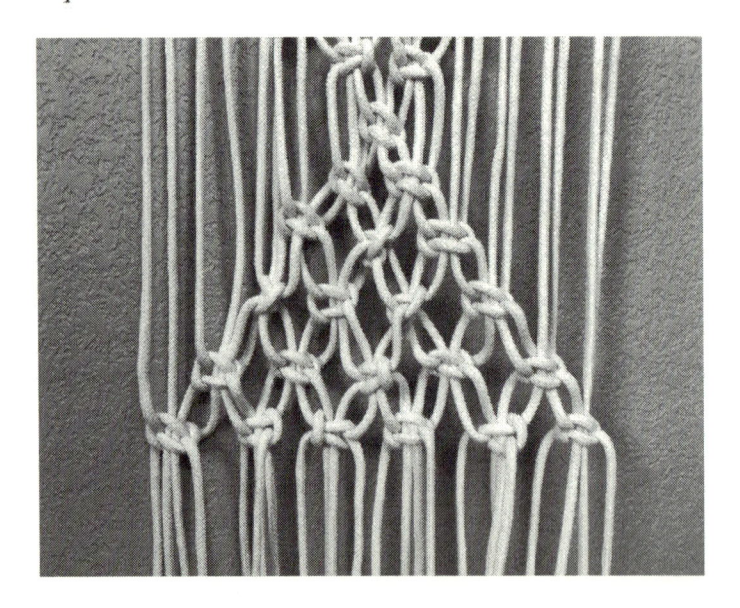

Time for more square knots! This time, we are going to be increasing them to form a triangle, or an upside down "V."

For the first row of this section, leave out the first eight and last eight cords. You'll make two square knots.

In the third row, leave out six cords at the beginning and the end. You'll have three square knots in this row.

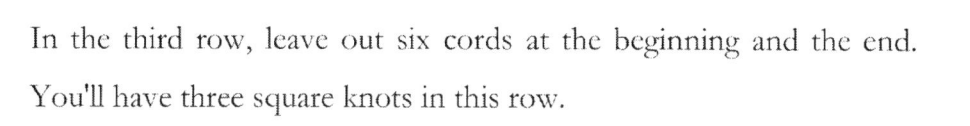

For the fourth row, leave out four cords at the beginning and four at the end. You'll have four square knots.

In the fifth row, leave out two cords at the beginning and the last two cords. Now you'll have five square knots in this row.

For the last row, use all the cords to make knots. You'll have six square knots for this row.

Trim and Knot

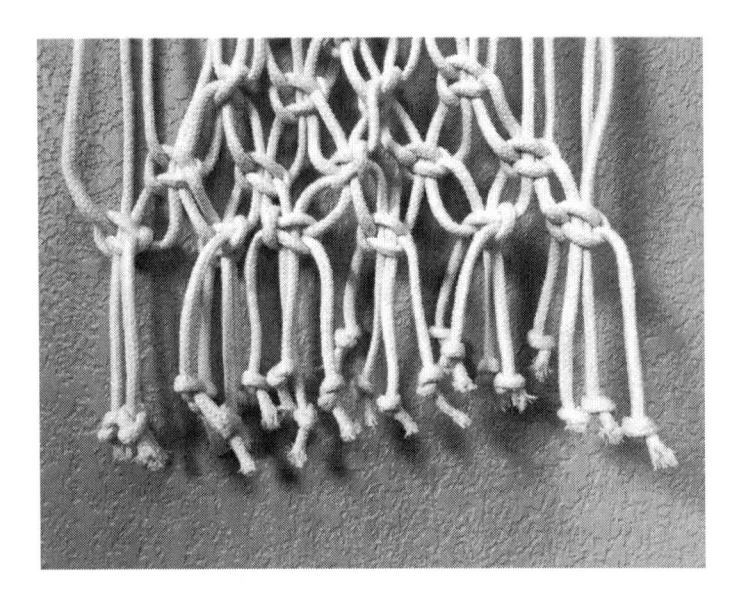

Time to give your macrame wall hanging a nice trim. Leave some space (about six to eight inches) under your final row. Use your scissors to cut the cords straight across.

You can leave it like how it is, add some beads, fray your ends, or tie simple overhand knots like above.

Macramé For Beginners

SIMPLE MACRAME TABLE RUNNER DIY

Macramé For Beginners

Supplies:

-12" wooden dowel

–22 strands of 16' cotton rope measuring 3mm

–over the door hooks

-2' of cotton twine for dowel hanger

-scissors

Macramé For Beginners

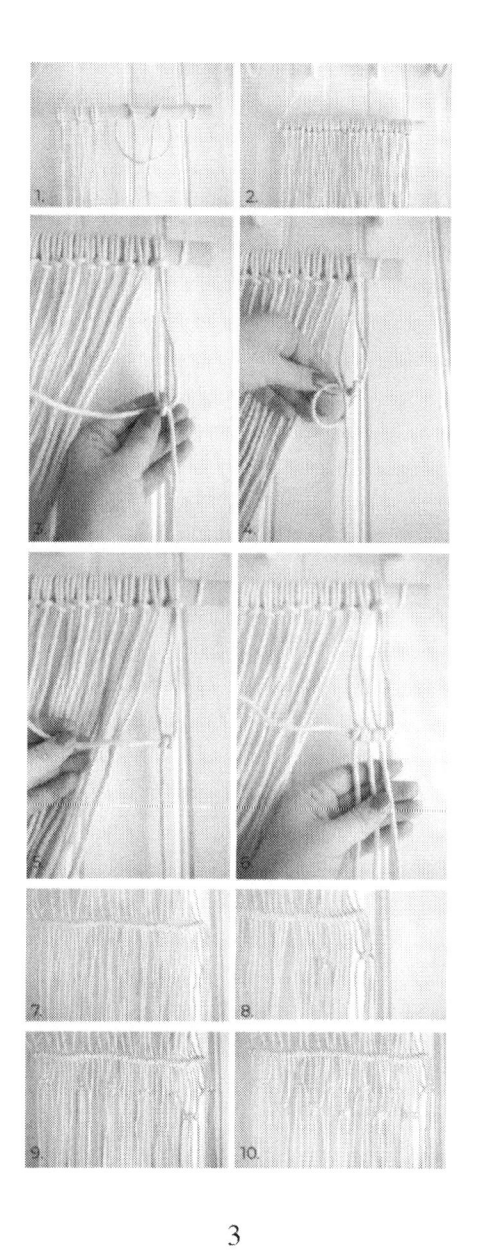

Step One: Tie cotton twine to each end of your dowel and hang it from your over the door hooks. Fold your first 16' strand of rope in half and create a lark's head knot over your dowel. See this post for even more detailed steps.

Step Two: Continue adding each 16' strand of rope using a lark's head knot until you have 22 total. This will give you 44 strands to work with.

Step Three: Pull the outer right rope across the front of all the other ropes (to the left) and drape the end on your door hook. This is going to be the base for the next row of knots called a half-hitch that will create a horizontal row. Use the second rope from the right side to tie a single knot around the rope you just draped across so that it's about 6" below the dowel.

Step Four: Use the same strand to tie a second knot over the base strand. This is called a half-hitch knot.

Step Five: Make sure they are even and consistent.

Step Six: Repeat with the second, third, and fourth rope from the outside and tie another half-hitch knot so that it's snug, etc. You'll start to see the pattern. This is a horizontal half-hitch.

Step Seven: Continue tying consecutive ropes in a single knot all the way across. You don't want this to be so tight that it pulls the width in at the edges.

Step Eight: Starting from the right again, use the outer four strands and create a square knot about 1.5" below your horizontal line of knots.

Skip the next four strands (five through eight) and tie another square knot using strands nine through 12. Continue skipping four, tying four until you get all the way across.

Step Nine: Starting on the right side again, use the four strands you skipped (five through eight) and tie a square knot about 3" below the dowel.

Step Ten: Keep tying the skipped sets of four strands in square knots until you finish that row.

Macramé For Beginners

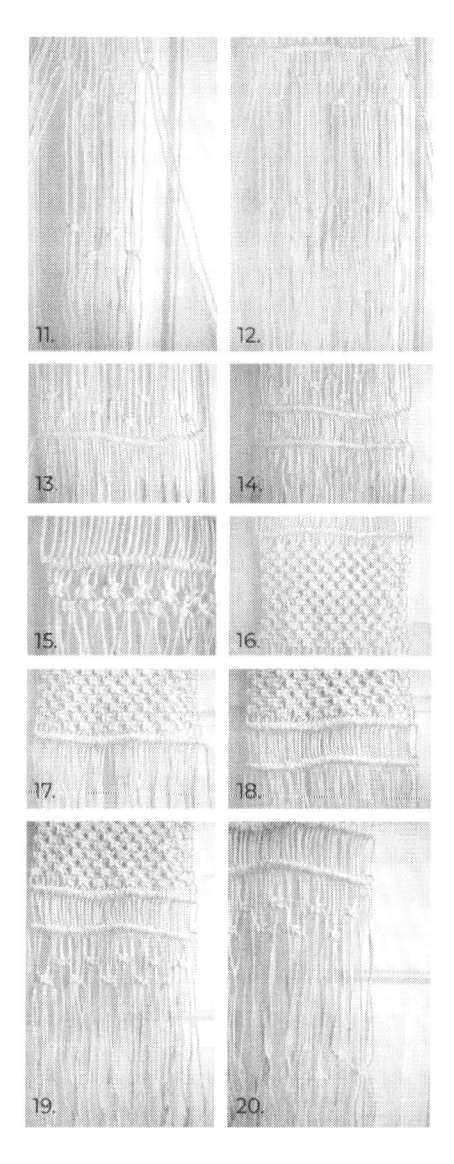

Step Eleven: Pull the outer two strands on the right side off to the side.

Then use strands three through six to create another square knot about 11" below the horizontal row of knots in step seven. Then use the next four strands to create another square knot about 1.5" above the last square knot.

Step Twelve: Continue all the way across as shown. You won't do anything with the last two strands.

Step Thirteen: Starting from the right side again, create another row of horizontal half-hitch knots by repeating steps three through seven.

Step Fourteen: Starting from the left side, use that same base strand of rope and create another horizontal half-hitch row of knots about 2.5" below the last one. You'll be working from the left to the right on this one.

Step Fifteen: Starting on the left side, create a row of square knots without skipping any strands that rests about 1" below that horizontal line of knots. Then create a second row of square knots by skipping the first two strands on the left before tying another full row of square knots. This is called an alternating square knot. You don't want much space in between these rows so you can pull them tightly together as you add each square knot.

Step Sixteen: Keep going until you have about 13 rows of alternating square knots total. This section is the center of your table runner so everything else from this point is going to mirror what you already wove above.

Step Seventeen: Add another horizontal half-hitch row of knots starting from the outer left side and working your way to the right.

Step Eighteen: Move down about 2.5" and use the same base rope to create another horizontal half-hitch row of knots that move from the right to the left.

Step Nineteen: For this section, skip the outer two strands of rope on the right and then tie a square knot using strands three through six. Skip strands seven through 10 and use strands 11 through 14 to tie another square knot. Repeat so that you're skipping every four strands. You'll have six strands left on the left side.

Skip rows one and two on the left side and tie strands three through six into a square knot about 1.5" below that last row of square knots. Then skip the next four strands and finish off the pattern for that second row of square knots. This will leave you with six extra strands on the right side.

Step Twenty: Measure down 11" from the last row of horizontal knots and tie a square knot using the outer four strands on the right side. Then tie the next four into a square knot about 1.5" above the last knot.

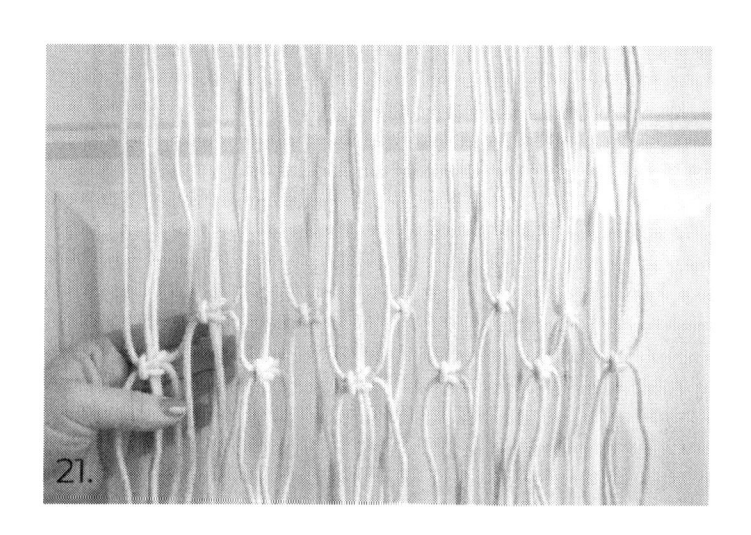

Step Twenty-One: Repeat all the way across.

Macramé For Beginners

22.

Step Twenty-Two: Finally, tie one last row of horizontal half-hitch knots about 1.5" below the row of alternating square knots. Trim up the ends to be as long as you'd like, making note of how long they are on the opposite end. Remove the cotton twine from your dowel and slip all of the lark's head knots off gently. Then cut the center of the lark's head knot loop and trim up the ends.

Now you're ready to set a very charming table!

The center of your table runner is the ideal spot for a centerpiece, so layer on a trivet and find some fresh flowers to help anchor your eye. You can even use it as its own giant placemat on a breakfast bar to make sure your kitchen is looking its best! You can also use the three simple knots you learned, the lark's head knot, the half-hitch knot, and the square knot to create a variety of textured wall hanging designs!

Macramé For Beginners

MACRAME PLANT HANGER DIY – A FRIENDSHIP BRACELET FOR PLANTS

Macramé For Beginners

To make the DIY Macrame plant hanger you will need:

Macreme flower pot

Spray paint

Cotton cording, rope, or strong rope-like yarn (which is what we used)

Scissors

Washi tape

Macramé For Beginners

To make the hanging loop for the macrame plant hanger:

Set the eight cords together and fold in half, so you have 16 strings with a loop top.

Tape 4 inches below the top of the loop. Take the 6' cord and tie it with a bay knot to the top of the loop.

With the right string knotted you can loop around the middle of the loop with a vertical bay knot: take the right thread over the loop, the under the loop, then through the thread and tighten. Then take the same thread, passing through under the loop, upward through the loop and pull at the thread through and tighten. Continue doing this knot until one half of the loop is done. Then take the left thread and do the same the other way.

Now that you have a nice decorative loop, removed the tape. With the remaining thread from the loop, tie together with a gathering knot. Twist the two lengths around the 16 long strings for at least an inch and tie to secure with a double knot. Trim the thread ends.

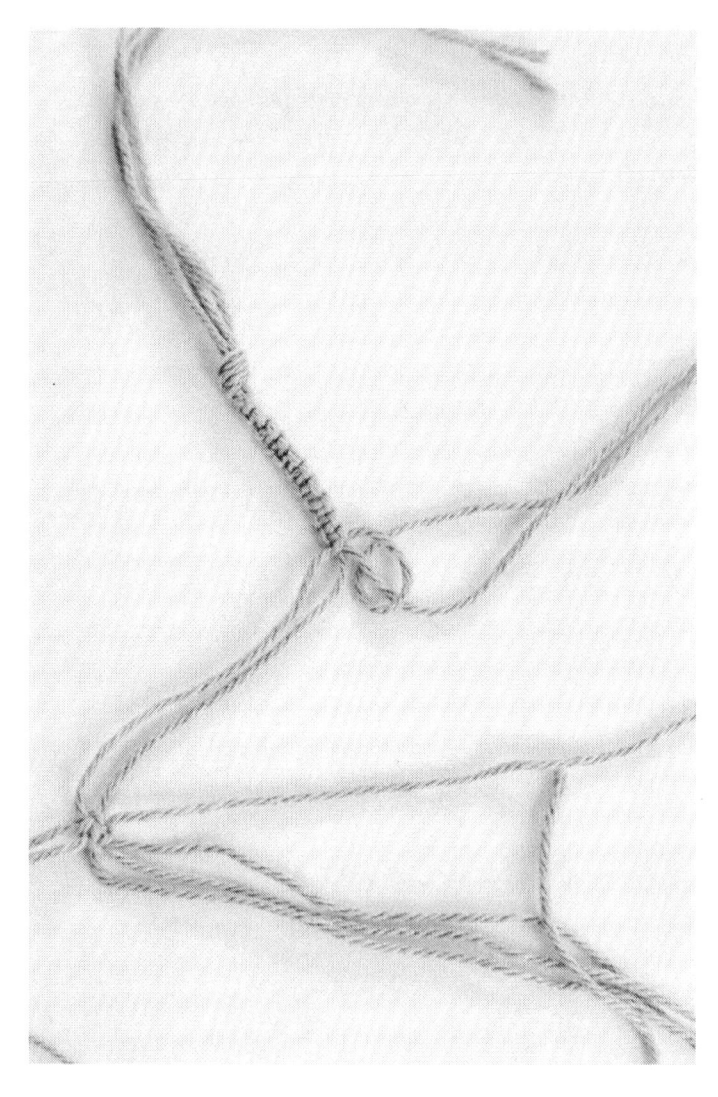

Separate the 16 strings into 4 groups of 4 to start knotting. In order to keep the long pieces of strings from twisting onto themselves we recommend wrapping the string into individual balls/bundles. Starting at the end of each string, wrap around the width of your hand a few times and with the remaining length wrap around that bundle leaving about a foot of string free. This takes a bit of time to organize all the strings but really helps things not get all twisted.

In one group, knot a long section with the wave knot. Continue for as long as you want. Repeat for the other 3 groups to ensure that the pattern is the same length everywhere.

Tie a knot in each section about 6" down.

Start tying the square knot. Repeat for the other 3 groups for the same length.

Now we will make the net portion that will hold the macrame flower pot: taking two strings from one group and two string from the group beside it, tie three square knots about 2-3" below that last knots. Repeat for the other 3 groups. Make sure that no strings cross over any strings and that only adjacent strings are knotted together.

Take two strings from one group and two strings for the group beside it again and tie three square knots 3" below the last knots. If your pot is large you can continue with this netting technique for one more round.

Macramé For Beginners

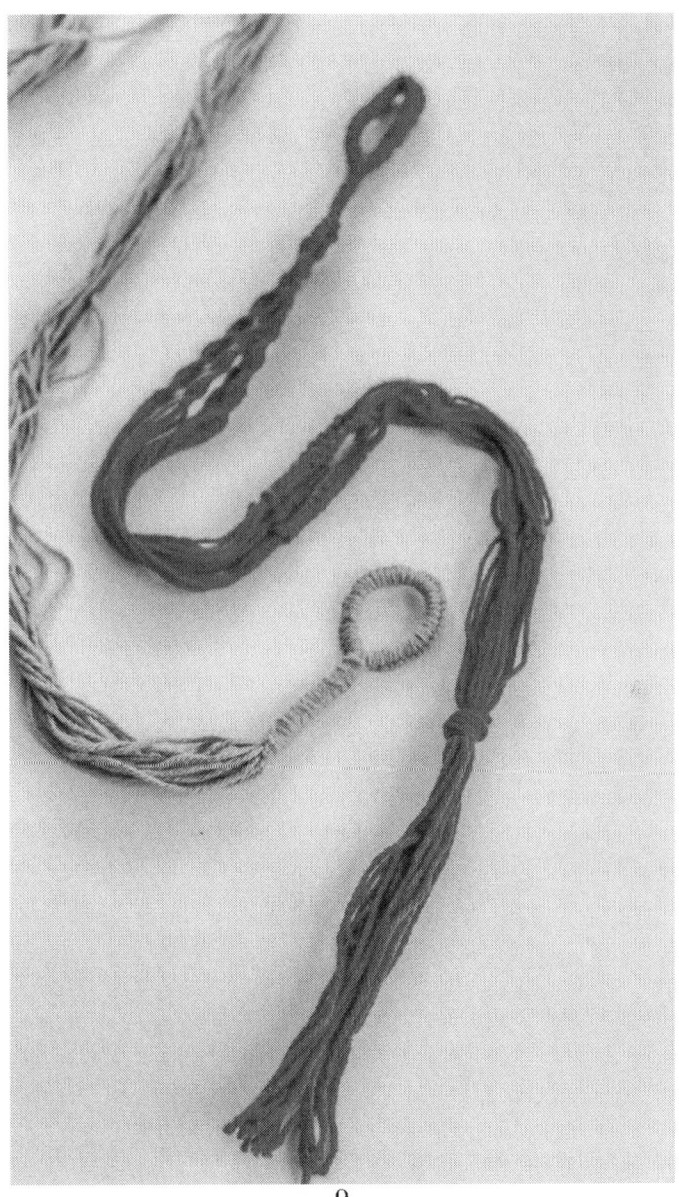

How to make a macrame plant hanger Once you are this far.... you have arrived at the end! Whoohoo! Now it is time to tie all the strings together in a large knot about a couple inches from the last set of knots. Trim the strings to make a tassel to finish off the macrame plant hanger DIY.

I love a craft that is fun for learning something new and also one that
I know I'll enjoy for years to come at home. These macrame plant

hangers brighten up the wall and bring a major dose of happiness to the space!

How to Make this DIY Macrame Tote Bag using Jute

This bag looks great styled up for summer, but it will also take you through autumn too. Imagine a few squash sitting inside as you head home to get cosy under a blanket with some kind of spiced drink. Am I giving you the autumn feels yet?

Materials

Jute Rope | Bag Handles

Macramé For Beginners

Instructions

Macramé For Beginners

1. Cut 10 lengths of 2.3 metre long rope. Fold them in half and thread the folded centre through the gap on the bag handle. Take the ends of the rope and pass them through the loop you've made in this previous step. Pull tight. Repeat this until you have 5 pieces of rope attached to each bag handle.

Macramé For Beginners

2. Starting at one end separate off two pieces of rope and push the rest to the side. We're going to make the first knot with these two pieces. This is the knot we'll be using throughout the tutorial, so if you get lost keep referring to the next few steps.

Make a bend in the right strand so it crosses over the left rope at a right angle.

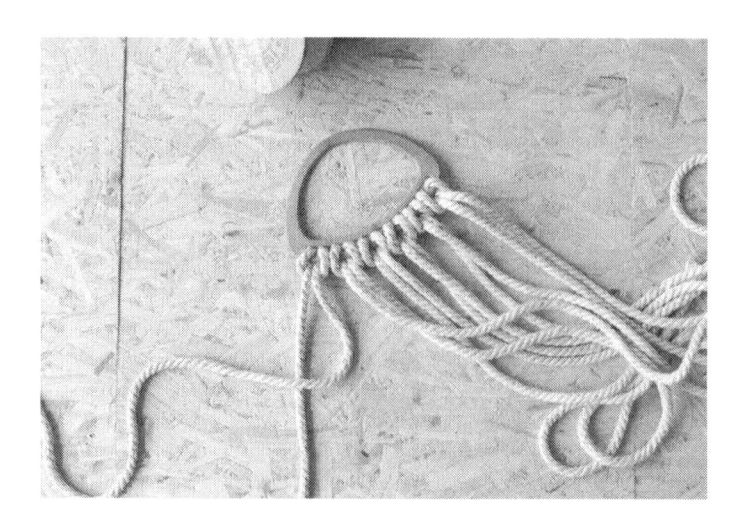

Take the left rope (which is still straight) and thread that through the space you've made with the two ropes. Pull both ends of the rope away from each other until the knot has formed and is in the right place. You want it to be about 5cm from the handle.

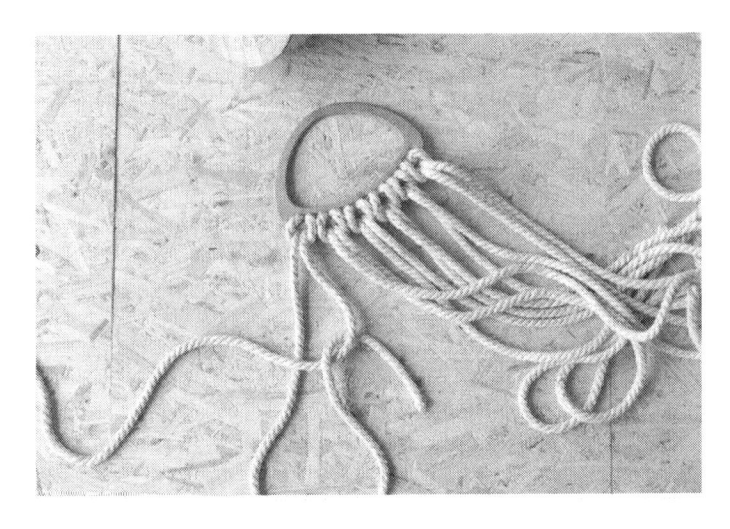

To complete the knot take the left hand rope and put it over the right this time.

Thread the right hand rope through the gap this time. Pull the knot tight again. This is now a completed double half hitch knot.

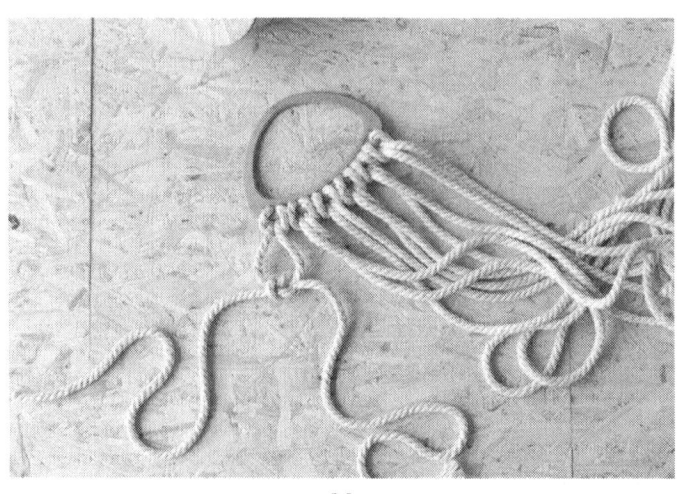

3. Make four more of these knots in a row using the rest of the ropes on the handle. Then start again, but this time miss the first rope and knot the second and third. Continue along the row. This time you will make four knots and the first and last rope will not be knotted.

4. Once you've completed the second row, make the third row the same as the first (so five knots, without missing any ropes).

5. When the third row is finished repeat steps 2-4 on the second handle. Once that's done bring the two handles together with the back sides facing each other.

Macramé For Beginners

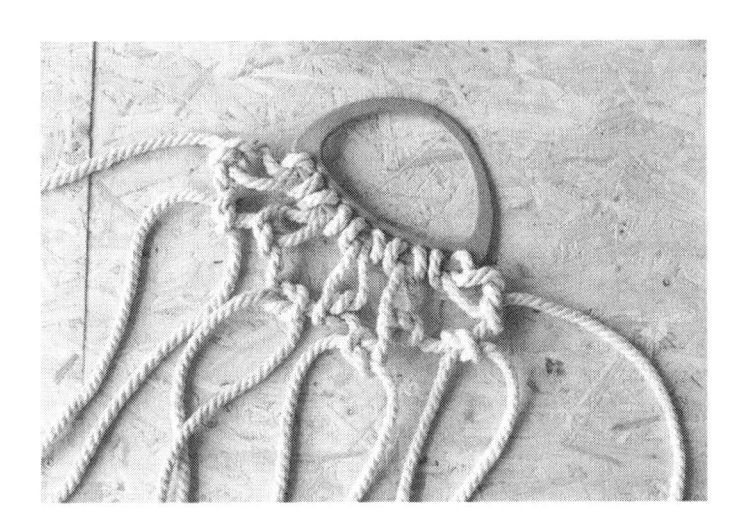

6. To start the next row take the two end ropes from both the front and back of the bag and knot these together.

Knot the ropes along the front and back until you reach the other end. You should then be left with the last ropes on the front and back.

Knot these together.

7. Keep knotting in this pattern until you have around 10cm of rope left on the strands.

8. Cut a length of rope 4 metres long. Tie this onto the last side knot using the same technique as you used for the handles.

Macramé For Beginners

9. Take one strand from the front and one from the back and wrap the rope around them. Tie one double half hitch knot then take another two knots (one from the front and one from the back) and do the same again. Work until you reach the end.

Macramé For Beginners

10. Untwist the rope that is hanging down. Tie strands of these together between knots to hold in place. You can add some glue to these to strengthen them. Comb it out to create a fringe.

And your bag is done. If you want something with a pop of colour try dip dying it in a natural burnt red or sage green. Right, I'm off to go buy some fruit and veg!

Made in the USA
Columbia, SC
24 November 2024